Healing With Shadows

ALSO BY
NIKIA LEOPOLD

POETRY

Dark Feathers
Small Pleasures
Swan and Jack-knife

FOR CHILDREN

Sand Castle Sea Horses
The Ballerina and the Gargoyle
Once I Was
'K' is for Kitten
Adam's Crayons

Healing With Shadows

Poems by Nikia Leopold

PINYON PUBLISHING
Montrose, Colorado

Cover Art by Giorgio Morandi, *Still Life of Vases on a Table*
(*Natura Morta di Vasi su un Tavolo*) 1931 etching, 249 mm x 336 mm
Courtesy of the Galleria d'Arte Maggiore, Bologna, Italy

Photograph of Nikia Leopold by Amy Macht

First Edition: January 2021

Pinyon Publishing
23847 V66 Trail, Montrose, CO 81403
www.pinyon-publishing.com

Library of Congress Control Number: 2020951561
ISBN: 978-1-936671-71-7

ACKNOWLEDGMENTS

My grateful acknowledgments to the editors of publications in which some of these poems appeared or are forthcoming:

Antietam Review: "Ars Poetica"; "Eleni"

The Baltimore Review: "The New Style"

The Christian Science Monitor: "Risotto"

Commonweal: "Escarpment from Water"; "Once More"; "The Phrase"; "Vacation"

Confrontation: "Song from Old Hawaii"

Ekphrasis: "Healing with Shadows"

Poet Lore: "Centerpiece"; "Child-Church" (Published as "Yellow Laughter"); "Silbers Pharmacy"

Poetry East: "Aunt Laurel"; "Natura Morta"

The Small Pond Poetry Magazine: "River Roads"

The Sow's Ear Review: "Family"; "Quince"; "Still Life"

Tar Wolf Review: "Close"

In memory of Bruce Carl Leopold

1944-2016

CONTENTS

III

IV

V

VI

"The cure for anything is salt water —sweat, tears or the sea."

—Isak Dinesen

I

LOSS

The cherry tree
ghosts my walk,
shrouding its house
with drifts of blossom,
weeping April away.
Each day I pause,
gauging its loss.

This morning heat rose
from the kettle, stirring
a cluster of capiz shells
hung from the sill—
thin discs,
clinks barely audible.

"Be gentle," they warn
my tough grievances,
"loss can hunt you down,
haunt you in the fall
of petals,
in your husband's long pause
before a response."

OVER

The moon is leaving
our gravity
and in a billion years will be
beyond our vision.
I put the paper down, try to imagine
A moonless earth …
No tides. No cyclic rhythms
to inspire us.
Will we breathe as evenly?
Will women bleed each month?
No tidal pools, no fringe of limpets,
urchins, tiny crustaceans, reveling
in a universe of pumice.
No sense of something always
traveling round us—a familiar—
like the cat marking her days
with a sequence of habitual places.
No presence to expect,
perhaps to worship.

When the moon finally floats
out of sight
I imagine a great
sigh
torn from earth's body.

PURCHASE

I've always been drawn to the phrase:
'Get a purchase on …'
It breathes of reach in every sense,
of grip and ownership.
"Sold!" calls the auctioneer,
"to the woman holding an orange cat."

A 'purchase' arrived this evening
through the slit of kitchen door:
last light grazed a leg
of your empty chair,
the scent of lilac crept to me.
Our cat lounged on the porch,
watching the darkening path.
All this, mine.

You are rarely still enough to grasp.
You're the puppet the auctioneer lifts,
limbs flailing,
and the seller himself.
You're Schrödinger's cat, purring in its box—
or not.
Don't come back.
Don't make me Sisyphus again,
endlessly trying to get a purchase
on your heart.

QUINCE

Sunken under the weight
of an old quarrel
our house settles in deadfall.
We float from room

to quiet room, I turning
a corner, drifting down a hall,
he lingering in the kitchen while I
skim by—both numb to everything
but this new cut in old scar,

until he stops, caught by a glimpse
of quince hedge through pocked glass,
buds clenched and red.
I slip in.
We watch, not touching, as

the buds open slightly, and
the house begins to rise.

RISOTTO

Beyond the kitchen window
white limbs of a sycamore
are swimming in the wind.
Threads of saffron stain
the grains of rice.
Stirring, I think of Leopardi's sweet
shipwreck in the depths of time and eternity.
My wooden spoon's the present to be licked,
the distant tree infinity to worship.

INTIMACIES

From our porch I hear
the beltway swarm
around its hive of city.
Before me, soft turf still
printed by a gurney.
One hornet's sting:
mayhem in his body.

In the waiting room
I wrote his name on
the back of a grocery list
till it was a thicket of lead.

A night of different intimacies—
cardiograms, an IV pole,
my role as supplicant
holding the rails
by his bed.

This morning he left
for work as usual.
Blessing of habit.
I walk to the wheel-ruts,
scuff them to dust.
The beltway hums
its foul music.

CRADLE THE DAY

whose faint light cries
to be held by anything:
brick walls, hollow trees,
even the steam
rising from my coffee.

Noon streams
illusions of youth.
Such benevolence lets
me miss everything
less,

lets me write about
the one unborn who slowly
bled to nothing.

My back is stiff,
my fingers smell of pencil.
Long shadows beard the lawn.

Cradle the day as it dies,
in the starry points
of elbow, wrist and hand.
Comfort it with simple songs

of soft brown moths,
smooth stones
and the stooping toward
an old man's
kiss.

STILL LIFE

Speckled brown, pure pale green,
round and oval, duck and swan
blown of their contents,
my weightless trove
from the Amish market.

The eggshells float in a celadon
pond. The bowl is flawed,
a chip on the rim.
The potter seemed surprised
when I chose it.

Reminders of my rifted family,
my unused womb.
With a glance, I heal the bowl's
cracked lip, thread a yolk
through each pinhole.

MORE

In their dark falling the flakes
made lovely havoc of us,
erasing the road,
conjuring a slow white inch
on the hedge.

Promise of more sorcery
as we went to bed.

Morning. The show finished.
Brilliant sun exposes
each wrinkle
in our long-married hands.

Wind flinches a branch—
glitter drifts
through scarves of air.
you gesture toward the window,
brushing my wrist,
at the promise kept.

II

VACATION

Beyond my pillow
the Arno
stalls.
Carp are still.
No current discloses
source from destination.
Spring and sea
pause
like two middle-aged
shoppers comparing
the virtues of
fresh water with salt.

My father once swam
in the Arno,
but, on vacation
from death,
I settle implacably
into the smooth sheets
of the present,
my old wishbones
content
to watch river-silk
wattle the ceiling.

SECRETS

Clouds low over the mountain,
sheep burring hillsides,
the Tiber swirls slowly
round Roman pylons,
and beneath Rieti another town—
Vespasian's bricks keep
damp red secrets
in the cellar
of our hotel.

In the piazza dusk
and fish-spine cobblestones,
white wine and ruby Campari
as the passeggiata flows
from narrow streets—
ardent couples, the very old—
this endless stroll, this stream
we float in for a while.
The evening churns
with murmurs and laughter,
swifts circle the bell tower
till it rings.

Later, in olive-dark night
I wake to your mouth on mine,
your body hovering over me,
and though I'm exhausted
something in this day, this place,
lets me rise to you
like a river,
offering secrets
I never knew.

"ANNUNCIATION"

Simone Martini, 1333

The letters fly straight to her,
thick gold insects
bypassing lilies in a gilded vase
to pollinate
the sallow flower
of her face.

She recoils
in exquisite disdain,
her pupils tiny weights
sliding toward the words.

He hovers,
half hawk, half angel
in fluttering plaid,
breath smelling faintly of rust.

No garden here, except the vase,
and over it an artichoke
of cherubim.

No flight of columns into distance,
no past to vanish in
or sky to breathe.

No openings for doubt.

These are early days.
The fastidious girl,
so graceful,

doesn’t know she has no shadows,
tucks herself into ultramarine,
thinks her robe’s a mountain
edged with curved gold swords.

She’s trapped in amber,
the words coming at her.

MONTE SOLARE

This ancient palazzo
is freshly restored:
a garden with delicate tendrils
frescoes the walls
of our room.

One blue butterfly
visits the bouquet
blooming over our bed—
I smile wryly at my fantasy
of conceiving a child
beneath the flowers.

Who stayed here first?
A maiden aunt, twin sisters?
Who opened the casements
each morning to glimpse
the olives' glittering leaves?

A few objects are displayed
from the time of the aunt,
the cousin, my favorite
a tiny iron
of great weight.

I want to believe
it was heated
in the bowels of the house,
hope that deep in the cellar,
fire still lives.

AT TWENTY

He was an architect
and our evenings began in the city.
Florence was earth to his Antaeus—
the power source.
With his arm possessing
my waist,
I learned its ancient grid.
Each detail of cornice,
texture of paving stone,
arc of bridge
renewed him as we walked.

Clink of scotch at a bar,
then his car and the curving viale
where he parked
and I learned
the province of man:
a vulnerable place
of tender roots, sudden fountains,
strange, dazed colors
that stained me woman.

I teased about our children's names:
"We'll call the boy 'Armadio,'
(Italian for 'wardrobe,')
and the girl 'Tessera,'
(meaning 'Tile.')
"Voglio quattro," he said.
('I want four.')

We parted in New York
after months of separation,
his gift of femaleness
bestowed with guilt on another.
Standing at the door, eyes lasers,
he squeezed my breasts goodbye
so hard I gasped,
head bent in shame.
Florence restored him.
After decades of marriage
I dream in his colors.

FAMILY

Walls of narrow streets
were neighbors,
facing windows borrowing
light, shade.
From our balcony
I noticed a bowl of fruit
emptying, filling,
on the table opposite.
Each night, over the sill,
a dishcloth, worn,
was spread to dry,
red stripes long faded.
Its people could
afford a new one,
but touch, close use,
had made it family.

Years later, unable to sleep,
I remember how carefully
the cloth
was offered to the air.

"NATURA MORTA"

Giorgio Morandi

Two tumblers, a vase, a canister
cluster before a pitcher,
simple forms on tan ground.
Nothing here's too proud
to share its shape,
to find a common line.
Lids slip together—
one creamy swath
binds two in rich economy.
The pitcher, copen blue, rises
in the center
like a Madonna of Mercy
gathering her folk, full and tall,
its handle a split heart
arcing into sky.

IN ROME AGAIN

Where the Spanish Steps
end, streets splay
like rivers
bearing luxuriant
boutiques on either bank:
Buccellati, Bulgari.

My goal is an anomaly:
Antichitá,
a slit between *Pucci*
and *Blahnik,* narrow
as a coffin.
The old man is there,
thinner, eyes clouding
to pewter.

His trade is time:
vintage Venetian glass,
mosaic boxes,
gilded Florentine trays.
I am overcome
by choice, heat,
my frayed Italian,
and an elusive scent.

He moves slowly
from shelf to counter.
Though he has a tremor
each item I've selected
is wrapped with respect,
secured by his seal.

As he hands me the parcel,
I recognize the store's
chaste odor of dried figs
to be my father's.
When he locks his door
for lunch I hope
he will walk toward someone
waiting at home.

SICILY, 1920

On her wedding night
Sofia bled to death.
Her bones were as delicate
as a pheasant's, light as sighs.
She married a burly youth,
and was gored
by his uncontrollable horn.

The sheet was hung
from their balcony,
soaked red.
Women closed their eyes,
stepping blindly.

The piazza sang of blood
from old men smoking pipes,
drinking grappa.
"I wish I had his brute,"
said one.
"It must have felt like entering
an angel, so pure, impregnable,"
mused another.

The sheet was Sofia's shroud.
At Mass the groom,
distraught,
could not fathom
why men kept clapping
his back,
as though he had sired a son.

HEALING WITH SHADOWS

'The Life of St. Peter,' Masaccio, 1427

Peter moves like a sleepwalker
down the ochre street,
eyes hollow with denying Christ.
He won't see the dun and salmon walls,
feel the warm dust on his feet,
hear the sighs of the crippled
who line his path.

But in his shadow's wake
the man with the staff
has already risen, and next to him
another with a bandaged ankle stands,
hands pressed in prayer.

Once there were no shadows;
all the backgrounds flat bright gold
to the edge of the world.
No life could root
in particular darkness,
swell into self.

Now it's the young one's turn,
squatting on stick-thin legs,
elbows resting on make-shift crutches.
He looks up.
Shadows flow from Peter's feet—
dark largesse
bathing the boy's shins and knees.
In a moment he'll walk.

Peter knows remorse
grows shadows so deep
they make us whole.
His sorrow stretches beyond him,
finding its own horizon.

III

CLOSE

Milkweed
drifting
between my parents'
deaths
like fine snow,
like a floater
in the eye,
a shallow moat
between dreams.
Am I lying
next to you,
Mother, buried
under the fig tree?
Or scattered with
you, Father, ashes
whitening
the lilac's leaves?
Close to you,
closed to you—
ashes and figs,
figs and ash
on the tip
of my tongue
through the morning.

SONG FROM OLD HAWAII

"I'm going to California,
when I come back we'll marry,
what shall I bring you?"
and she answered shyly:
"A hat, that tilts,
and shoes, high-heeled,
a petticoat, with lace,
and a dress that clings,
and clings, and clings."

How graceful my young mother,
dancing this antique hula,
singing in her low voice.
The couple's courtship,
so innocent, so matter-of-fact:
promise, give, take, come back—
even a child could understand it.

My husband went to Wyoming
this morning, to be with his father
who can barely breathe,
his leaving a reminder, a precursor
of all loss.
He held me silently,
promises, presents
unneeded in a long marriage.

VISIT

Father requests
more butter for his pancakes—
ten years of death
have whetted his appetite.
"More bacon, too, darling."

I'm delighted to see him:
stubbly chin, curved fingernails.
His dry humor emerges
from the maple syrup—
I bend to kiss his head.

"Happy birthday," he says,
"What's your pleasure?"
"I want to be three again,
and for you to hide
the peanut butter."
He nods and I slip

into the small apartment
of childhood,
where each day began
with a hunt
for our favorite treat.

The curtains whisper
as I fumble among sunlight
and gauzy folds,
finding the jar as always,
holding it up unsteadily
to his ancient love.

AUNT LAUREL

In the nursing home,
how small you seem,
centered on the bed,
exuding a peculiar charm.
You wish to face the window.
An aide lifts your stiffness—
limbs frozen—all of a piece—
and then I grieve for you
who had a wealth of choices,
and for the cat I lifted once
from a country road, its mate
lingering by the rigid body,
bones light as driftwood
in the moonlit field.

ELENI

Past the chickens,
up wooden stairs
to the room
with a Metaxa bottle
on the mantel,
and on the bed
an old woman
swaddled in black.

My newly met cousins
are proud:
"One hundred and two
and still enjoys her food."

Like a jay her questions
pierce, repeat:
"Who **are** you?
Who **is** it?"
My answers flutter her face,
but she is deaf,
and blind.

They tell me some nights
she shrieks to get her bearings.
I see the shrieks flicking
out the window
like bats,
over the coop,
down the slope
settling in the olive grove.

Is she Tithonus
begging for death,
or merely a crone
needing her brandy?

My eyes, reflected
in the blind ones,
are bright with fear.
I will myself
to sit beside her,
placing an arm
around her carefully.
What if she flinches,
a fury in bird bones
screaming "You will be me!"

She lifts a veined hand—
thin parchment—
trembling it down my face
to shoulder and breasts.
"Woman, a woman!" she cries.

I nod 'yes' with my body,
whisper her name, "Eleni,"
Till holding is cradling,
till it's time for her lunch
and for us to retrace
the wooden stairs.

THE CANDY-MAKER

As I swim in a lilting sea,
sunset appears—two thick bars—
orange and gold like the treacle
my grandfather used.

He left Sparta at 18,
learning in La Jolla
to make fondants and fudge.
There he found my grandmother.

Taffy was his specialty.
Soon he pulled in anger from
the wife who mocked his accent,
his Hellenic Bible. Later, he left her.

We never met, but I imagine him
stretching this evening's richness
to transparent caramel
with deft veined hands
to please the child I was.

THE NEW STYLE

She never wanted to weave it anyway,
that shroud for her father-in-law,
and every night, when Penelope
undid the web
it was a twice-sweet secret.

She was clear-headed, of course—
on Ithaca everything's seen
through a crystal of salt.
Still, alone in darkness, she felt
even death could be postponed.

The sea helped
through her long effort—
its ebb and flow echoed
the rhythms of the web,
let doing and undoing seem natural.

The pattern was in the old style,
the only style: geometric.
If a suitor glanced at it
there was no way
to tell progression.

When Odysseus came home,
his wife began to hear the lays
swirling around him,
snatches of song about Circe and Calypso
and Nausicaa of the lovely thighs.

She was moved to weave again,
and worked into the night
while her husband waited
in the bed of olive wood
he'd made for them.

She wove Elysian asphodel—
buds, pale shoots, fields in full bloom.
It seemed such a tender invention:
blossoms, not abstractions.
No one guessed they grew from bitterness.

ISLAND

He's walked into town
for who knows how long,
and I consider
easing my desire.
No. I'll wait, be faithful.
But I'm sunburned and it's hot,
too hot even for the thin
nightgowns I brought,
and I lie carelessly,
limbs splayed like a starfish,
one shaft of light through
a louvered window,
the only sounds waves
and the whir of a ceiling fan.
I think of his hands
as the rhythm of air stirs me—
slowly the fan becomes my lover.
For the first time
I understand those old myths—
how a woman might be taken
by anything: a breeze,
a shower of gold.

ESCARPMENT FROM WATER

Land-scent sweetens salt
with waves of beach plums
and succulents.
From the lapping water
a dazzle of sea grape
leaves and sun
on the ridge.

The reef is a face of mouths
urged in tufa
by insistent whispers of the sea.
Ceaseless catechism has made
the rock eccentric,
its porous surface
a wilderness for hermits
wearing borrowed shells.

In alcoves, urchins meditate
upon the blackness
of their spikes.

The waves rise, and in recession
all the rock
is iridescence, bubbling
raw orange, aqua—
algae, refreshed
by the tidal question.

I face a niche,
breathe
with waves and beach plums,

bathe in the glitter
of salt and sea grapes—

tread water
as long as I can.

THE PHRASE

Sometimes, traversing a day,
the phrase arrives:
'My kind father.'
I pause, go on,
knowing this is a way
we're remembered.
Nothing specific,
nothing planned or sacramental,
no sacrifice of a pure white goat,
just this small tide that rises,
slipping over the basin's lip
onto a dry patch of my life.

IV

ARS POETICA

"Lots of colors first,"
my godson reminds me.
Green, yellow, red, purple …
simple shapes, contingent.
We crayon till the white page
becomes some early world—
continents before they drifted.

"Now black over everything!"
Fingers slick with wax,
we bury the colors alive.
Nick takes a paper clip, unbends it,
etches a planet, then two moons
of unearthly orange and blue.

My turn.
Tight curls peel to each side,
revealing, bit by bit, violet tulips,
trees with heart-shaped leaves,
and in the center,
an awkward bird of paradise.

As we put away the crayons,
I heard her round green song.

I hear it now, sometimes,
this buried song,
and know the bird is shining
in her sketchy plumage,
raising her bill
to scratch the black above.

CHILD-CHURCH

Black ice! the car slides,
then rights itself.
I continue slowly to the school,
remembering dreams I've read of—
angels whispering different routes,
escapes into Egypt.

I urge the children's minds to wander,
escape into themselves.
I ask them not to rhyme,
ask them what the moon sounds like.
'Cymbals,' they write, 'dust falling,'
'talking chalk,' 'snow-bells.'

So long ago my world was simple.
It lived under the card table
beneath a green cloth Mother flung
to the four flat ends of earth.

In that dim child-church
I could believe anything:
that paper dolls had souls,
that nicknames kept me
from the grove of goblin-trees.

"What are *you* like?" I ask the children.
'I'm like a pond, clear and calm.'
'I'm a little gift shop in the city.'
'I'm the roof protecting my family.'

I've learned that nothing hides us
except ourselves,
no angels whisper.
But we can play a little—
this evening I saw black branches
split the sunset
into orange laughter.

RIVER ROADS

Our neighbor, in retirement,
cultivates a plot of words.
He attends to them lovingly,
searching round roots,
transplanting his findings
to index cards.

He presents one each Friday
with a tone of challenge:
"Arrive."
I try it softly on my tongue
but miss its origin, chagrined.

Pleased, his gift intact, he says,
"When this word was forming
the forests were so dense
rivers were the only roads:
one **arrived** by the **river**."

I pour our coffee. In its steam
the forests rise, trees massed tight
as hairs of the wild boar—
blue-green, immense, deep-stocked
with amber and shadows.

A river meanders within—
'S' of an unknown alphabet,
bearing skiffs of pelted barbarians
whose gutturals rasp its banks.
Tributaries join,
escorted by a panoply
of raucous, lustrous crows.

Archie waits until the forests disappear,
the amber and the river are well-stored.
He takes a sip of coffee,
smiles, then offers
"Tribe."
I tap my cup,
urge the answer to arrive.

SLEEPING ALPHABETS

In the forest, alphabets are waking.
An 'A' stands,
swaggering on wide-set legs,
letters follow, join the battle cry.

Another, brandishing its serifs,
dances fiercely through a thicket,
rejoicing in the ligatures.

One grows deep.
Each letter now a tree:
'A' fir, 'B' birch, 'C' hazel.
Old roots stir, twitch,
eager to entangle.

Bones of letters
gleam from shallow furrows.
Vowels sigh in evening mist.

Over field and forest
stars will rise, endlessly patient,
writing, rewriting their fiery primers.

At night perhaps the sleeping alphabets
forget their differences:
eons of bloody tongues.

Perhaps they return to each other,
murmuring common words:
'ox,' 'snow,' 'ash,' 'brother,'
dreaming past sign to meaning,
past bone to soul.

'Heart,' 'eye,' 'thunder,' 'fire.'
Each one a talisman,
each a clearing
that lets some starlight in.

GYPSY SPRING

There were rumors you were coming:
castanets of cracking ice,
fringes of light through the hedge,
peepers foretelling your rhythm.
When the caravan arrived
the shock of your laughter
broke into crocuses.

Your passionate dance
made the koi leap high,
made tulips fill their cups,
and lilacs keep their
purple promises.

I opened my life to your riddles:
You will lose a wing and rise.
You will find the worm of eternity.
You'll fall in love again
with the precise and invisible.

Your light-fingered breezes stole my sleep.

Now you've broken camp, moved north.
The azaleas are felted by rain
like a heart cramped with loss.
If I'd crossed your palm with silver
borrowed from this swollen moon
could I have bribed you to stay?
No. You'd go anyway, incorruptible,
leaving a handful of petals.

ELDER

Age has made me
delicate.
Thinning skin reveals
violet veins,
wrinkles fine
as craquelure
on a quattrocento
fresco.

How cautiously
I move
to keep my balance—
small stuttering
steps
like geisha
in tiny
embroidered shoes.

My swollen hands
tend
what they can,
scattering nuts
for squirrels,
kibble for koi,
seed
for sparrows.

I wash myself
with care,
each crease laved.
The trio of

hair whose odors
once beckoned
are scentless
sachets.

Layering days
clothe me
in a host of patterns.
A sleeve's fold
holds
a thousand tears,
a world
of sweeping touch.

“SILBERS PHARMACY”

in dull gold letters on the cornice.
A corner store, windows stretching light
into the streets’ blackness.
Promises on a purple banner,
blue and red drapery, apothecary jars
glowing like stained glass.
Is Mr. Silber sleeping, or downstairs
in slippers, ministering to the old man
with a persistent cough?
The draperies obscure them
while light keeps breathing through
colors hinting at celebrations, births,
the shop a match struck against
our death-day—that unknown day
we think of most.

After Edward Hopper

MARKET

An old woman moves toward me,
using her cart as a walker,
head hunched
into fragile shoulders.
I see her often here,
respect her painful travel
through the aisles,
her persistence wearing a groove
in her wake.
This time, as we pass,
the lane pulses
with invisible ripples—
all the breathing and choosing,
reaching and stooping
of those past, those to come.
I grip my cart, one with all of them.
Melons, lemons, color and order
have lost their power to soothe.
I study my list,
matching word to thing.
At the checkout
my name is unfamiliar,
but I smile the usual 'thanks'
and 'take cares,'
crafting my own rift
in the air.

WAITING

I never looked at him closely,
afraid of his eyes,
of his torso
set flat on a board
in front of the department store.
But I wanted to give his monkey,
in its tight red sweater,
a quarter,
wanted to feel the animal's quick
dry fingers scrabble against mine,
hear the 'clink' in the cup,
say its name: "Giuseppe."

The escalator's rubber rail
was a jugular swallowing, curving
us to the second floor
where an old man in black tie
played a baby grand, "Deep Purple"
mingling with mysterious bells
as Mother chose her cologne.
Then my treat: an ice cream clown,
cap the cone, vanilla face the scoop,
smile a sliver of candied fruit.

Always the man waiting,
the eager monkey hand.

CENTERPIECE

Wooden tiers spin madly
flogged by angel candles.
Shepherds circle,
crooks frowning over
lacquered sheep,
tiny mandarins
made in Taiwan.

With each rotation
the apparatus squeaks
like a plaint of earth
chafing on its axis,
echoing the cries
of what it bears.

Little toys surround the mobile:
a snowman dreaming
in his glass prison,
a crystal tree,
and armless Jack, out of the box
sequined collar winking
round his fixed red grin ...

Cross or solstice can't heal him,
or make us kind.
Still, each year I light
the angel candles,
watch their flames circle
this absence of miracle.

COMING BACK

You had the brass
to make things happen,
even when we were ten.
Hairpins tossed from the balcony
onto your parents' patio
as they entertained in summer,
landing softly, subtly,
on napkins, lettuce, laps.
Sometimes you spat.
When your mother raged
toward our room you said,
"Switch beds!"
She left, embarrassed,
after pummeling the guest.

At eleven you initiated sex.
Sleepovers thrilled as we posed
flat chests for imagined boys.
What stories you began
about seduction and I spun on,
still ignorant, evading
the ultimate act with
'Came the Dawn.'
Soon we were practicing the twist,
debating the depths of sin
in a French kiss.

You took tap, ballet,
strong curved calves
launching you into the air.
You never seemed to land.

Your husky voice
sang us into whatever heaven
you wished.

Broadway, films, cabaret.
You began to fast within the feast,
full features thinning, agile body
living on itself,
clavicles a nervy necklace
you wore with pride.

We fought:
"Eat anything, *anything*!"
Sometimes you put the phone down
gently,
sometimes not.
Then you fell and broke your thigh.
You chose your own exit:
in your own bed as you slept,
all sixty pounds of you.

My consolation: we still speak often,
telling our love.
"Earthy sprite," I whisper,
"Come to the kitchen,
slip through the window-crack.
I'm alone, drinking amaretto."
Here you are,
relaxing with the hand-blown glass—
swirls of gold and amber.
We clink. We sip, we kiss.

And 'Came the Dawn,'
you're gone,
a hairpin left on your chair.

KWAN YIN

April, and the Goddess of Mercy
has arrived, presiding over our
living room from the mantel,
ebony robes swirling calmly,
head turned slightly to the right,
smooth hands overlapping.
My parents found her a lifetime ago,
and now they are gone.

Our family had few icons,
no crucifixes but in books.
I saw the Grünewald first at five,
shocked by the puce agony
I kept secret, along with the bulging
cod-pieces of striped silk
worn by men staggering
in an "Apocalypse."

Kwan Yin was poised in a niche
near the book that burned,
the one I tried to keep shut.
When I couldn't check my lust,
inviting infinite shame
into a single small body,
she kept her eyes lowered
and was always there.

Curved folds lapped her bare toes,
gathering about an essence
which I sensed but couldn't grasp.
Now, when I know the air

we breathe is laced with cruelty,
she has come home to me,
serene, shining, her tranquil smile
ever comforting.

HOLDING OUR OWN

Tonight the moon is one straight line
met by a pure curve like a rune
carved deep in the heart.
I still remember the black-haired boy
who read me poetry when I was sixteen.
Once, as we slow danced, I startled
at the thrust of his tongue.

Now time's thrust, its careless hooves
gallop through the body's garden,
cropping its pleasures, muddying
symmetries, moving on to another plot
while the moon watches,
secure in its ancient stance.

When I was eight I saw you, Marcel Marceau,
smiling sadly through thick white powder,
a living corpse
dancing with a phantom partner.
I remember your moon-face set against
an invisible wind,
moving ever forward in place.

VI

ONCE MORE

The full moon rises
at the top of our street,
a gradual discovery
made together
settling in.

Each month the moon
floods the boards
of our bedroom
floor with silver,
bestows a simple chair
with onyx shadows.

For thirty years
we've been moon-proud:
a glow within,
until his illness.
Now we are hushed, thin—
hoping for one more
fullness
together again.

TOUCH

He lies on our bed,
reading about the Civil War
for distraction, as, face pinched,
severe, he endures
the cancer that will end him.
I wonder if the theme
relates to his warring cells
but can't ask;
death's court is too formal.
I weep silently.
He grows weaker,
the hospital bed
and morphine come closer …
Our cat lies near him
as is his wont.
This morning I notice
he's stretched one hind leg
to rest on the crook
of my husband's arm.
They've fashioned a calm,
a space that eludes me.

BLIND MOON

Sun passes
through flawed glass
in the attic,
hushed
as my elderly cat
tracking its warmth
on padded paws.

The muted glimmer
of paperclips
from a plastic box
on my desk
communes
with a silver frame
holding his photo.

Black enters
by the windows, suffusing
my silent bedroom.
Now I revisit
that night of a blind
new moon

when after a month
of suffering, of cries
he couldn't contain,
I slipped
the wedding ring
from his finger.

EXPIRATION DATE

Entering the empty kitchen,
my ache turns to tears.
I consider
the medicine left over,
forgotten by a hurried
hospice nurse.
Ignoring my husband,
his body still warm,
I rushed to squirrel
the windfall
of morphine and pills
in the back
of a guest room drawer.
This treasure
keeps me safe enough
to face the counter,
make a salad,
and eat.

SILENCE

in my house
is no longer golden,
but this morning
light gilds the walk
and roams through
fireplace ashes
untouched
since his death.

Sun has bleached
one side
of the Navajo rug
we brought home
from our honeymoon.
Its rich reds and greys
cleave to the wall.
Some things persist
that are deeper
than silence.

CHANT

A steamed
artichoke,
one willow-ware plate,
one bowl.
No butter, no salt,
no sound but my breathing.
I peel the leaves,
scrape them between
my teeth, mind chanting
'He loved me,
but now cannot,'
as each drops into the bowl.
I savor the wedges
of heart slowly—
the day's meat, its intimacy.
'He was,
but is no more.'
On dusky paws
our blind cat finds her way
through the door.

DONATION

For eight months
I've been unwilling
to give
his clothes away.
August, and I sweat
among slumped
black bags,
one too full to knot.
I empty its excess
exhausted, bending,
struck by the memory
of Proust's
Françoise, cursing
a chicken
she's trying to strangle:
"Die, you bastard!"
I twist the bag again,
and tie with a surge
of betrayal.

THE CLOWN

A clutch of metal soldiers
lies in frozen battle,
sprawled on my desk,
waiting to be untangled.
The castle is stately,
deftly sawed and painted
by my husband's father—
drawbridge, turrets, crenellations,
irresistible invitations to play.

Sun splashes over the army,
finding the crimson grin
of an anomalous clown,
stretching his blue bloomers
up toward the flutes of his collar.
Why is he here—
entertaining the troops
or something more subtle,
hinting at how
one cell can change
among a host of others?

VANISH

Pages shine in my hands
as I read before bed,
the rest of the room
is dark.
When I turn out the light
fiction vanishes—
I'm left
with his absence
aching in my throat.
So many nights I fall asleep
light burning on a book
spilled from upturned palms.

OFFERINGS

In sleep I struggle
to slip
from his absence.

Each dream insists
he be there.
It's been a year

and still he offers
an iris,
a spray
of eglantine.

I wake to the sun
of ownership
for an instant

before my shadows
stir,
stunning me again
with his loss.

NOW

Grasping a banister
I hear the brush
of his wedding ring
on my forefinger.

In the quince hedge,
finches are chattering,
urging me out
to feast on red buds.

SPIRIT

The spirit of death
watches me try
to fill my life
with scent of lilac
and linger of cardinals,
last to leave at sunset.

I want to love again,
to touch a man's face
with my fingertips until
gentleness isn't enough.

The spirit eats silence,
licks the quiet,
feasts on my slender
chances for music—
my breath to quicken
with a man's song.

SAFE

When the last cat
had to die,
my house was empty—
nothing to love,
to take care of.
Husband gone first,
now our small family.
I came home to furniture
and the radio.

Tonight I turn
it off—
food and politics
an uneasy fit.
Click of cutlery
interrupted by chirps:
swifts newly hatched,
safe in the chimney wall,
back again.

Their parents brave
the dark tunnel
to feed them—
the shaft they will learn
to fly up
toward dazzling sky.
Not life I can tend,
but attending, just now,
seems enough.

www.ingramcontent.com/pod-product-compliance
Lightning Source LLC
LaVergne TN
LVHW050936080826
845145LV00004B/1289